I0710951

Instructions For The Raising of Pheasants

by Vermont Dept. of Fish and Game

with an introduction by Jackson Chambers

This work contains material that was originally published in 1922.

This publication is within the Public Domain.

This edition is reprinted for educational purposes
and in accordance with all applicable Federal Laws.

Self Reliance Books

Get more historic titles on animal and stock breeding, gardening and old fashioned skills by visiting us at:

http://selfreliancebooks.blogspot.com/

Introduction

I am pleased to present yet another title on Raising Quail.

This volume is entitled "Quailology" and was published by Fred Kerr in 1903.

The work is in the Public Domain and is re-printed here in accordance with Federal Laws.

As with all reprinted books of this age that are intended to perfectly reproduce the original edition, considerable pains and effort had to be undertaken to correct fading and sometimes outright damage to existing proofs of this title. At times, this task is quite monumental, requiring an almost total "rebuilding" of some pages from digital proofs of multiple copies. Despite this, imperfections still sometimes exist in the final proof and may detract from the visual appearance of the text.

I hope you enjoy reading this book as much as I enjoyed making it available to readers again.

Jackson Chambers

Preface

THE time has arrived to assist our native upland game birds by introduction of a new species in Vermont. Bad breeding seasons, disease, and a constant increase the number of bird hunters—these are three things which combine to make the natural propagation of grouse far more uncertain than it was twenty years ago. The artificial propagation of our own ruffed grouse is held to be an impossibility, and the only solution to the problem now before Vermont sportsmen lies in the introduction of a hardy strain of pheasants. By providing a supply of these birds longer periods of protection may be given the ruffed grouse without subtracting from the total quantity of bird shooting now enjoyed by the sportsmen, and a new and valuable species will also be added to our list of upland game birds.

The greatest difficulties will be encountered during the period of introduction. Methods of hatching and feeding will need to be studied, and ways found to protect the pheasant from natural enemies and from unscrupulous poachers, but it is hoped that the sportsmen will unite in their efforts to assist this Department until the new bird is thoroughly established and able to adapt itself to our natural conditions. Success will not come suddenly and completely, but slowly and surely, and as a result of hard work and cheerful co-operation among all those who are interested in the continuation of our wild life resources.

Five facts should be kept in mind:

(1) Pheasant propagation under artificial conditions presents no great difficulties.

(2) The pheasant is not injurious to farm crops; rather the bird has a direct beneficial influence in destroying harmful insects.

(3) The sex markings of the pheasant are so distinctive that the hens can be protected during open seasons and only male birds shot.

(4) Clubs, individuals or communities which assist in the propagation of these birds will receive the full benefit of their own work, as the pheasant has a tendency to remain in the locality where it is liberated.

(5)   The success of the pheasant enterprise depends
entirely upon the effectiveness of local protection and
interest.

With every hope that the coming years may see the
pheasant as much a part of our rural scenery as the
ruffed grouse now is, this pamphlet, the first of its kind
published in Vermont, is sent out to those who wish to
cooperate in this important work.

H. P. SHELDON,
Commissioner.

INSTRUCTIONS

N applicant having received notice that he is to have a shipment of pheasant eggs should proceed as follows:

When eggs are received, they should be put in a cool place of even temperature. This condition can usually be found in a cellar. Place eggs in a dish or tray filled with sawdust, dry sand or oats, turning them twice daily (morning and evening) until they are set. It is best to set eggs as soon as possible after receiving them.

If possible, it is best to provide a coop as described in the pamphlet issued by this department, but in case this is not convenient, a small box or coop such as a farmer uses for the rearing of chickens will do. The coop should have no bottom and should be placed on the ground. It is best to place coop out-of-doors somewhere in the shade of a tree or hedge where the hen will not be disturbed by other fowl and where it is as quiet as possible.

Provide a setting box about 16″x 16″x 6″. This is just a form having no bottom. Fill box one-third full of moist earth. Hollow this slightly by pounding. Next, place fairly coarse straw within the frame, shaping slightly and lining with soft hay or grass, but remember that the eggs must lie practically on the ground. The nest should have a very moderate incline toward the center. When eggs are found piled on top of one another when the hen is taken off it usually means that the nest is too deep. A nest nearly flat makes it easier for the embryo chick to break away from the shell. Eggs in any type of nest should be sprinkled with tepid water in very dry weather. A little Persian Insect Powder applied to the lining of nest will help to keep lice and mites away. Only Persian Powder, (Pyrethrum), which is procurable at any drug store, should be used, as powder containing carbolic is very dangerous.

If possible, secure a hen that is gentle and of light weight. Place the hen on some dummy eggs for a day or two and when satisfied that she will set steadily, place fifteen to eighteen eggs under her. Before setting a hen on pheasant eggs, she should be dusted with a reliable insect powder to destroy vermin. This should be repeated three times during incubation, but *never after eighteenth day* as powder will choke and kill the little birds.

Setting hens should be fed hard corn and should have plenty of water. Oyster shells and grit must be supplied as well as dry earth for a dust bath. The hen should be allowed to leave the nest for about twenty minutes each day. During this time any broken eggs should be removed and all soiled eggs cleansed with a warm, damp cloth.

It is best not to feed a setting hen from the time the eggs begin to pip until she is placed in the rearing field. Do not remove shell as the chicks come out, as these sharp edges keep the hen from setting too heavily on the newly hatched chicks. It is best to have full confidence in the hen and let her alone for twenty-four hours after pipping starts.

The chicks should be allowed to remain under the hen for twenty-four hours, then taken with the hen to a coop in a field near the house. The orchard makes a very good place for rearing young pheasants. The same coop used for hatching may be used here. Place coop on high, warm ground that is well drained, as dampness and cold are very fatal to young game birds these first few days. Three boards, one foot high, should be placed in front of coop so as to form a pen, using front of coop for one end of pen. Remove any long grass blades or weeds within coop and pen. Be sure there are no small holes through which the chicks can escape. It is necessary to keep them from wandering away from the hen before they have learned her call, which takes from two to four days.

On the fourth day, remove the boards from front of coop, still keeping the hen in coop. From this time on, and as long as the hen is confined, the coop must be moved to fresh ground each day. It is absolutely necessary that young pheasants have fresh, clean ground. After tenth day, release the hen, allowing her to range at large with her birds that they may be able to catch the many insects which it is necessary for them to have. The hen will usually return to the coop each night, but if she does not, don't worry, as she is sure to have found a better place close by. A shallow pan of water with pebbles in it should be kept in the shade near coop. IN NO CASE TRY TO CONFINE THE YOUNG BIRDS AFTER THE FOURTH DAY, AS THEY WILL SURELY DIE IF THIS IS DONE.

It will not hurt the young birds if they get some dew in early morning. When two weeks old they are able to stand any amount of wet weather if not exposed to the full force of a hard shower and if they have a dry coop as a shelter. They are hardy, and when five weeks old are fully feathered and able to take care of themselves.

Young birds should be fed as soon as they are removed from the nest. Only a small quantity of food should be given—never more than the birds will eat up clean. Any food left on the ground is harmful to young birds. It is best to place some of the food within reach of hen as it helps her to teach the chicks to come to her call. She also will clean up food left by her brood. DO NOT OVER-FEED. This is important.

The first week the little chicks should be fed four times a day. The food should consist of hard-boiled eggs chopped fine and mixed with an equal amount of slightly moistened stale bread or cracker so as to form a crumbly mash. One boiled egg will provide four meals for fifteen chicks the first week. It is well to mix in a little green food such as lettuce, watercress or tender clover, chopped fine—also a little fine grit once a day.

The second week commercial chick grain may be added to ratio. Reduce to three meals a day. These can be given as follows: *Morning meal:* chopped boiled eggs mixed with an equal amount of slightly moistened bread or cracker crumbs to the consistency of a dry

crumbly mash. *Noon meal:* chick grain moistened
with water. *Evening meal:* hard-boiled egg mixed
with moistened bread or cracker, and one or two
handfuls of chick grain. If crackers are used be sure
they contain no salt.

When birds are two weeks of age the egg food may be
gradually discontinued until at the age of four weeks the
food may consist entirely of the chick grain. The young
birds are very fond of curd (cottage cheese) and this
may be fed quite often. Clean water should be provided at all times. In feeding, it is a good plan to place
the food on a clean board. This must be cleaned thoroughly after each meal. When six weeks old birds
will be fully feathered and able to find food for themselves.

Feed the mother hen a small handful of whole corn
daily. This will keep the hen in good shape and will
also keep her from eating the food provided for the
little birds.

For All Birds—Young or Old.

Feed dutch cheese, or curd, and sour milk three or
four times a week. They like it and it keeps them
healthy, but be sure there is no salt in it.

Keep clean fresh water before them.

See that they have grit, oyster shell and charcoal. A little charcoal in their mash is good.

Green food such as lettuce, onions, beet tops, cabbage, chopped burdock and pig weed is good for them and they enjoy it.

A little beef scrap strengthens the young and the old birds and takes the place of bugs they may lack, but be sure it is sweet.

Do not feed more at one time than they will clean up, as it will sour and, if they eat it later, it will make them sick.

SHIPMENTS OF YOUNG PHEASANTS.

In addition to distribution of pheasant eggs, it is the plan of the Department to send out limited numbers of young pheasants from the State Game Farm. These shipments will be made in two ways: (1) broods of about fifteen young pheasants with hen foster-mother in same crate; (2) consignments of young pheasants which are old enough to take care of themselves.

In either case the applicant should remember that pheasants are very shy and should not be handled more than is absolutely necessary. The birds must be liberated immediately after being received.

In case of hen and brood, liberate at once in an open field near a piece of woods at least one-fourth mile from any building. Place the crate on its side, remove cover half way and allow hen and chicks to leave the crate of their own accord. A handful of grain should be scattered and the hen left to call her brood together. It is well to throw a little grain occasionally where the hen and brood were released. This will usually bring them back to same place for food, giving the persons interested an opportunity to watch the little pheasants grow and develop.

Well grown pheasants should be taken at once to the cover in which it is planned to liberate them. Before releasing the birds, scatter grain on the ground where it can be easily found. Place the basket on its side, slide the cover back about six inches, stand back and wait for the birds to come out, which they will do in a leisurely manner. After the birds have become accustomed to their surroundings the crate can be removed.

Address all communications to WILLIAM H. MORRILL, Department of Fish and Game, *Montpelier, Vermont.*

HELP WILD LIFE

to do its bit

BIRDS MAKE AGRICULTURE POSSIBLE.

BY KILLING INSECTS AND RODENT PESTS, THEY SAVE CROPS WORTH MILLIONS OF DOLLARS.

FISH AND GAME FURNISH FOOD.

THOUSANDS OF TONS ARE TAKEN ANNUALLY.

Conservation Laws are designed to make Fish and Game and Birds more abundant and are vitally necessary for National Welfare.

THE MAN WHO ILLEGALLY TAKES GAME OR FISH OR KILLS BIRDS DECREASES FOOD RESOURCES AND DEFRAUDS HIS COUNTRY.

REPORT VIOLATIONS TO THE NEAREST GAME PROTECTOR.

FISH AND GAME DEPARTMENT

of

VERMONT

The game is owned by all the people
and the ninety per cent or more of the
population who do not shoot game,
must still assist in protecting their
rights in the game and their right to
leave a heritage in wild-life.

HAYES LLOYD